GREEN BEAR FOR PRESIDENT

By Dang.

This Book Belongs to:
You and Me
and the
KidTime Family

Acknowledgments: KidTime StoryTime, My wife and kids. Eliana's "chocolate Green Bear story."
Art References: whitehousemuseum.org, Wikipedia, wamu.org, Franklin C. Courter.

Everything you can imagine is real. - Pablo Picasso

THE WHITE HOUSE
WASHINGTON, DC 20500

For: Mr. Green Bear
KidTime StoryTime Lane
Southern CA 91234

Scan QR code with your phone to read along with our video!

Green Bear is a little bear with big dreams.

Someday, I'm going to be President of the United States of America!

He also has a terrific imagination.
One day Green Bear imagined...

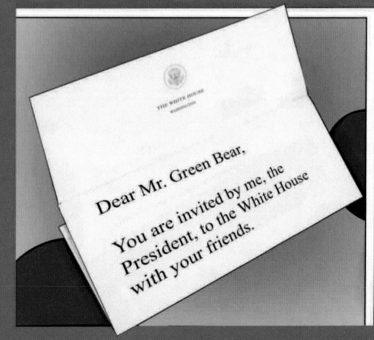

The day finally arrived and they took a taxi,

an airplane,

and a bus.

They all got on at the New York
Ave Station,

and took the subway to the White House.

At the White House they were welcomed and quickly brought to a special stage in the Rose Garden.

Green Bear wondered what was going on, and then he looked at the bottom of his invitation.

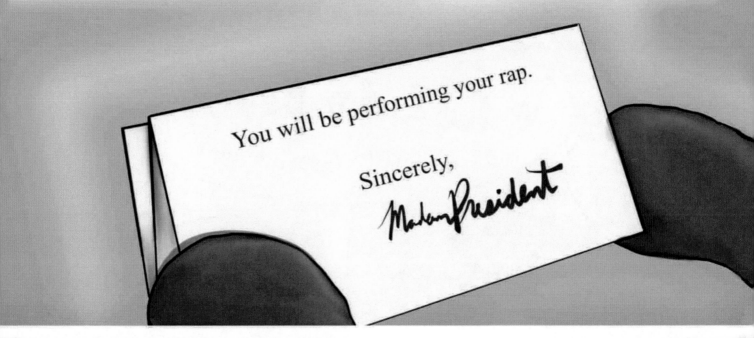

Everyone went onstage.
Green Bear grabbed the mic, and then...

The crowd loved it!

Scan QR code with your phone to sing the AlphaRAP with Green Bear

After the performance, the President came on stage and said:

Green Bear was so excited to start being President
As President, I will first appoint my staff. Doug, will you be my Chief of Staff?
Yes Mr. President, but ummm, what do I do?
Chief means you're in charge of my cabinet....just make sure that there's enough chocolate and stuff like that.
Ohhh, okay I will go make sure there are chocolates in the cabinet.

President Green Bear appointed his friends as:

There was one thing Green Bear wanted to make sure he did as President... give a speech.

Everyone went inside, but Green Bear didn't know where everyone was supposed to go, so he said...

Let's see how many of Green Bear's friends you can find hiding in the White House.

13

And then Green Bear found the Lincoln Bedroom

*Fun fact: Lincoln never slept in this room, he actually used it as an office.

20

And in the GREEN ROOM, there was a fancy luncheon prepared for President Green Bear.

Green Bear went to the West Wing to get some work done in the Oval Office.

The President has the power to veto or say "no" to legislation or laws that Congress wants to pass.

He can also sign legislation into law.

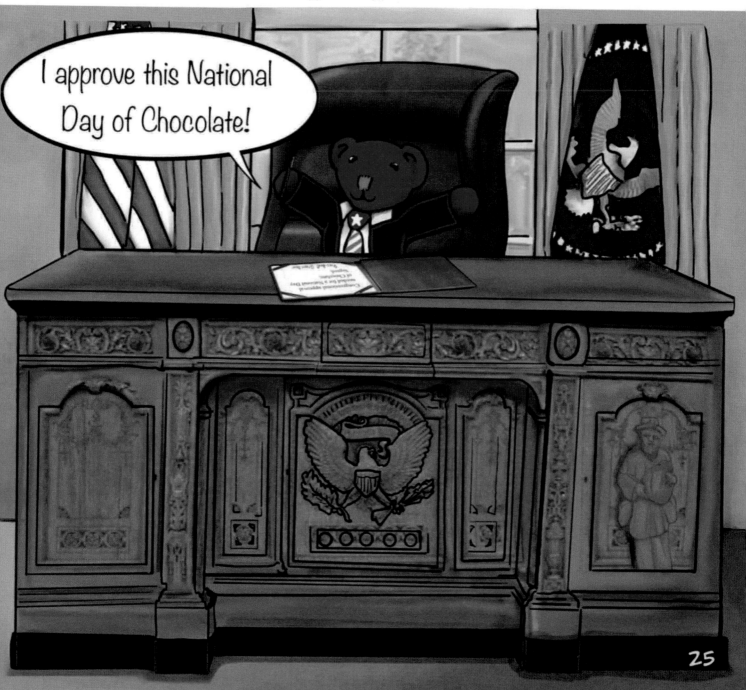

Then Green Bear went to his press conference where Red Bear had uncovered the pool in the press room.

After playing hide and seek, it was time for Green Bear's speech.

Green Bear then wrapped up his day with a Presidential Party!

It was finally time to go home.

This is what would happen if Green Bear were President. What would you do?

Abuela Bear's Chocolate Chip Cinnamon Cookies

I CUP SOFTENED BUTTER
I CUP WHITE (GRANULATED) SUGAR
I CUP LIGHT BROWN SUGAR PACKED
2 TSP PURE VANILLA EXTRACT
2 LARGE EGGS

3 CUPS ALL-PURPOSE FLOUR
I TSP BAKING SODA
½ TSP BAKING POWDER
I TSP CINNAMON
I TSP SEA SALT (OPTIONAL)
2 CUPS CHOCOLATE CHIPS (OR CHUNKS)

Mezclar todo junto

te amo por siempre,

Abuela

INSTRUCTIONS

- Preheat oven 375 degrees F. Line a baking pan with parchment paper.
- In separate bowl, mix flour, baking soda & powder, salt, & cinnamon.
- Cream together butter and sugars until combined.
- Beat in eggs and vanilla until fluffy.
- Mix in the dry ingredients until combined.
- Add 12 oz package of chocolate chips and mix well.
- Roll 2-3 TBS of dough into balls and space 2 inches apart onto pan.
- Bake in preheated oven for approximately 8-10 minutes.
- Take them out when they are just BEARLY starting to turn brown.
- Let them sit on the baking pan for 2 minutes before removing.

Learn more about the White House and see if you've found all of the hidden KidTime StoryTime characters.

Page 13

The Diplomatic Reception Room is an entrance to the White House from the South Grounds. The panoramic picture is called "Views of North America" (Circa 1961).

Green Bear, Pink Bear, Red Bear, Tibby, Hooty, Doug (putting chocolate in a cabinet) White Rat, Fuchsia, Witcheficent, & Olivia.

Page 14

The Game Room is where presidents play pool. Fun Fact: Abraham Lincoln was a self-confessed "billiards addict."

Dill, Tibby, Random Rooster & Gilles

The Workout Room was converted from a sitting room by the Clintons. It had also been a room for housekeepers.

White Rat & Twotone Cat

The Solarium is a popular room of the first families. It has been used as a hangout, a sleeping porch, a place to BBQ and a school (for the Kennedy children).

Doug, Green Bear, Corny & Dill

Page 15

The Lincoln Bedroom (office):

Ghosty, Green Bear, Collie Dog, Doug.

Page 16

The Theater Room was converted from a long cloakroom in 1942, the room is occasionally used to rehearse major speeches, like the State of the Union address. But more often it is used to screen movies by the first family and guests, often before they are released to the public.

Olivia, Storyteller, Tibby, Abuela Bear, Green Bear, Hooty, Gilles, Doug, Red Bear, Pink Bear, and Dill

Page 17

The Flower Shop is used to arrange fresh flowers for the White House.

Corny

A Bowling Alley was installed in 1947 for Truman's birthday (fun fact: he didn't like to bowl). There's been one ever since.

Green Bear, Doug, Dill and Random Rooster

Page 18

The Chocolate Shop is where chefs make amazing treats like the annual Christmas gingerbread (white) house.

Doug, Witcheficent, Gilles, Abuela Bear.

Page 20

The Green Room is where James Madison signed the first declaration of war (of 1812) and was named the "Green Drawing Room" by John Quincy Adams. This room has hosted a lot of history.

Dan G. (the author), Tibby (painting), Green Bear, Lamby, Random Rooster, Doug, Red Bear, Pink Bear, Olivia, Gilles, Abeula Bear

Page 24-26

The Oval Office is the president's formal work space. Prior to 1902, most presidents worked out of the Lincoln bedroom. It's current location was established in 1934 to accommodate FDR's wheelchair. The "Resolute Desk," pictured in this book, has been used by most modern presidents, and does, in fact, have a secret panel in front.

Page 24: Doug, Green Bear, Fuchscia Fish, Page 25: Woody "the old man of indeterminate origin" in the desk wood. Page 26 Dill & Gilles

Page 27

The Situation Room is a part of the West Wing designed by JFK to funnel important sensitive information to the president to help him in matters of protecting the United States.

Dill, Witcheficent, Snakey, Green Bear, Curious Jorge, and Pink Bear.

Page 28-29

The Brady Press Briefing Room was the location of an indoor pool (built for FDR) until Nixon had it covered over to accommodate the needs of the press corps. Named for James Brady, Reagan's press Secretary who was shot and crippled.

Dill, Red Bear, Tibby, Fuchsia, Octavius, Green Bear. Page 29 Green Bear, Hooty, Dill and Tibby.

Page 30

The East Room is a ballroom and banquet room used for many functions. The Famous Stuart painting of George Washington is found in this room. During the Fire of 1814, First Lady, Dolley Madison made sure this was saved from the flames of the British fire.

Olivia, Hooty, Dill, Fuchsia, John Travolta, Princess Diana, Storyteller, Doug, Twotone Cat, Abuela Bear, Tibby, Octavius, Witcheficent, Pink Bear, Red Bear, Gilles, Random Rooster, Corny, and Green Bear.

Page 32

On board Air Force One:

Dill, Doug, Witcheficent, Green Bear, Abuela Bear, Corny, Olivia, Gilles, Hooty, Red Bear Pink Bear and Storyteller.

Visit: www.kidtimestorytime.com
https://www.youtube.com/@kidtimestorytime

DAN G. IS AN AUTHOR AND ILLUSTRATOR WHO LIVES IN A BROWN-ISH HOUSE IN IDAHO. HE LOVES LEARNING, DRAWING, BAKING COOKIES AND TELLING STORIES.

WHAT PEOPLE ARE SAYING ABOUT "GREEN BEAR FOR PRESIDENT."

This is the Book of my LIFE!
No seriously, it really is.
-Green Bear

Two bear claws up.
– Pink Bear and Red Bear

Dramatic!
-Olivia

It's horrible! Except for the BAT STEW!
-Witcheficent

Eee eee eee, it's so cheesy, Eee eee eee.
-White Rat

I love it so much!
-Doug

Made in the USA
Las Vegas, NV
17 March 2023

69230347R00024